The
Celts

Leonie Pratt
Designed by Zöe Wray
Illustrated by Terry McKenna

Consultant: Dr. James E. Fraser, University of Edinburgh

Reading consultant: Alison Kelly, Roehampton University

Contents

3 Iron Age Celts

4 Meet the tribe

6 High on a hill

8 Village people

10 Farming and food

12 Looking good

14 Crafty Celts

16 Gifts for the gods

18 Festival fun

20 Fearsome fighters

22 Telling tales

24 Trouble ahead

26 Battling Britain

28 Celtic clues

30 Glossary of Celtic words

31 Websites to visit

32 Index

Iron Age Celts

The Celts were people who lived in Europe over 2,000 years ago. They lived during a time called the Iron Age.

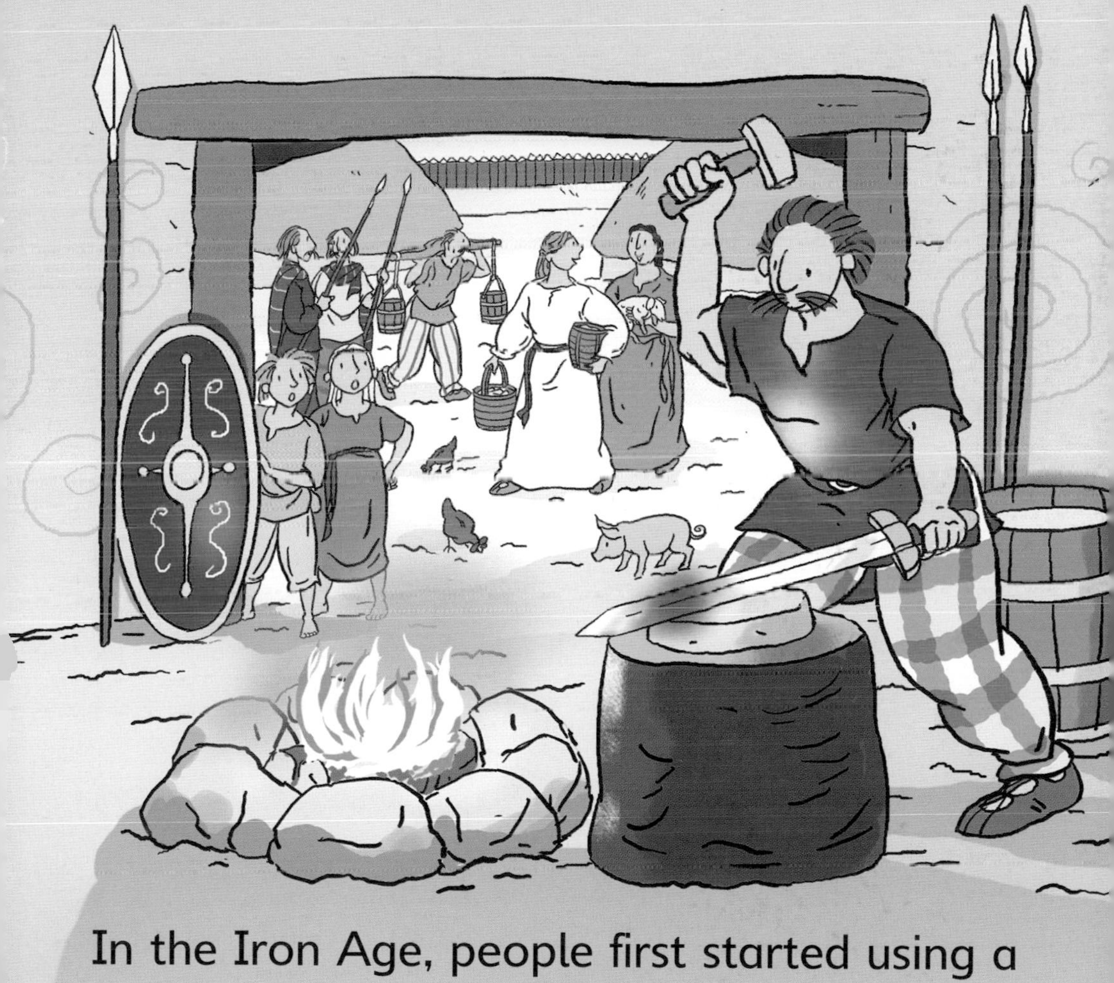

In the Iron Age, people first started using a metal called iron to make tools for farming, and weapons such as swords and spears.

Meet the tribe

The Celts lived in groups called tribes.

The tribe leader was a chief, a king, or sometimes a queen.

The best fighters in the tribe became fierce warriors.

Bards told stories and poems about famous warriors.

Druids were priests. Everyone thought they were very wise.

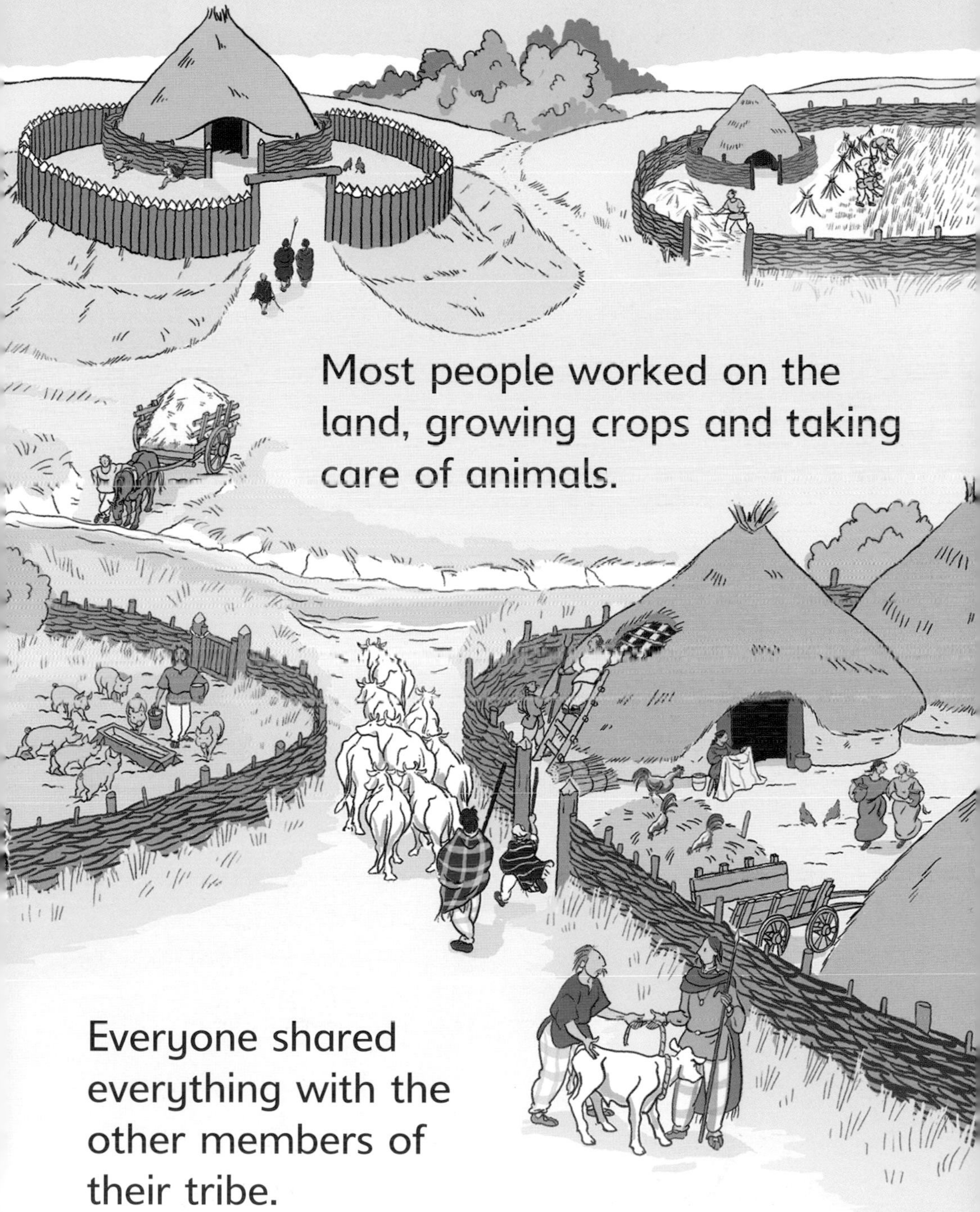

Most people worked on the land, growing crops and taking care of animals.

Everyone shared everything with the other members of their tribe.

High on a hill

Different tribes didn't always get along. They often tried to steal things from each other, so many tribes built forts on hills to stay safe.

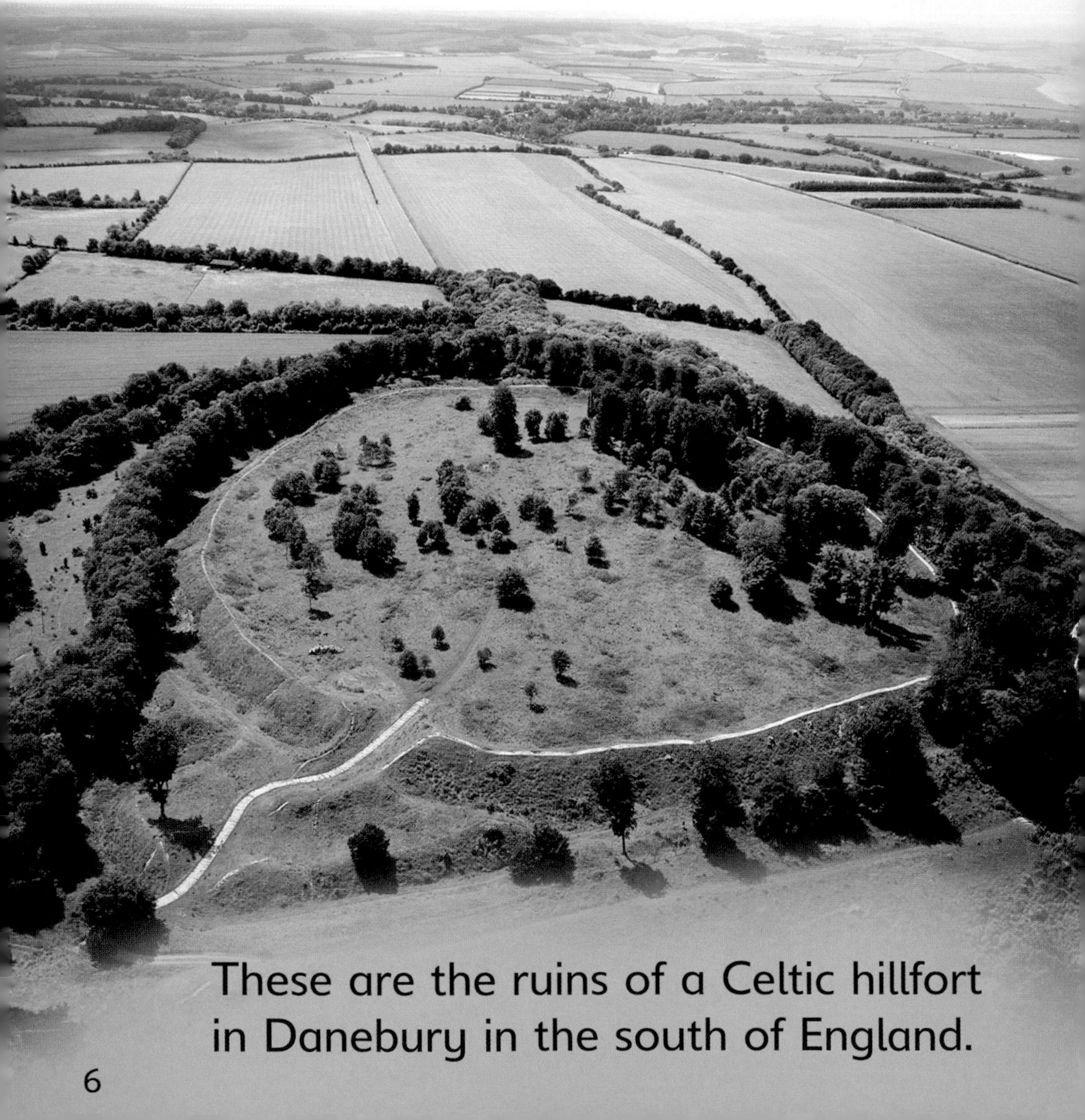

These are the ruins of a Celtic hillfort in Danebury in the south of England.

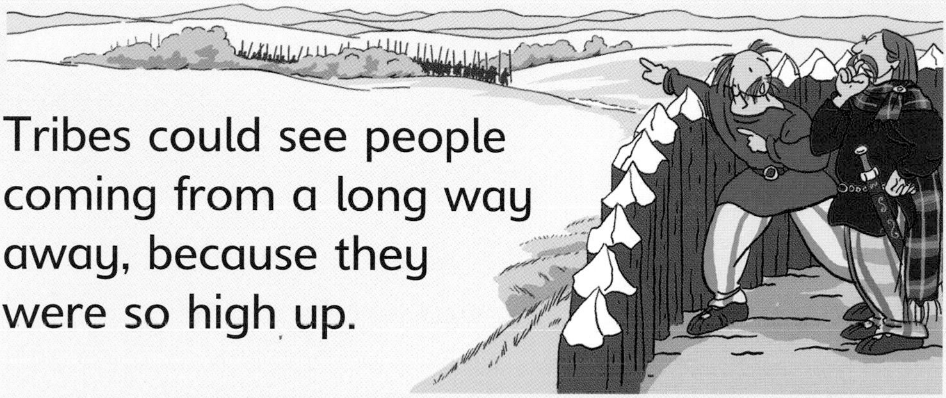

Tribes could see people coming from a long way away, because they were so high up.

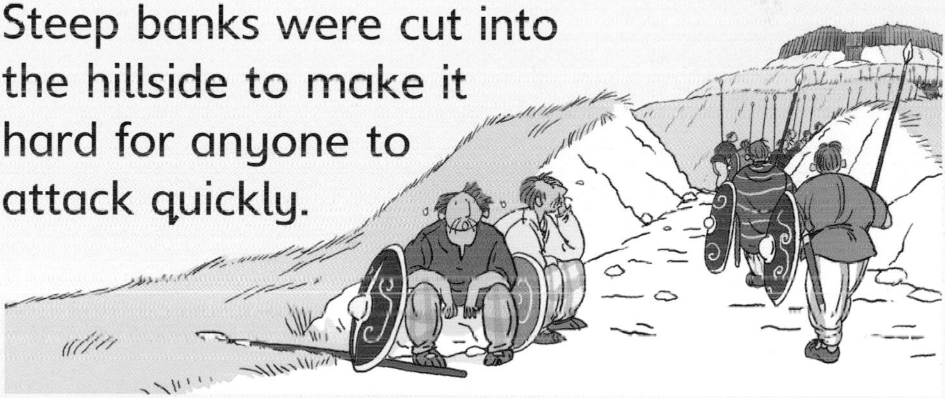

Steep banks were cut into the hillside to make it hard for anyone to attack quickly.

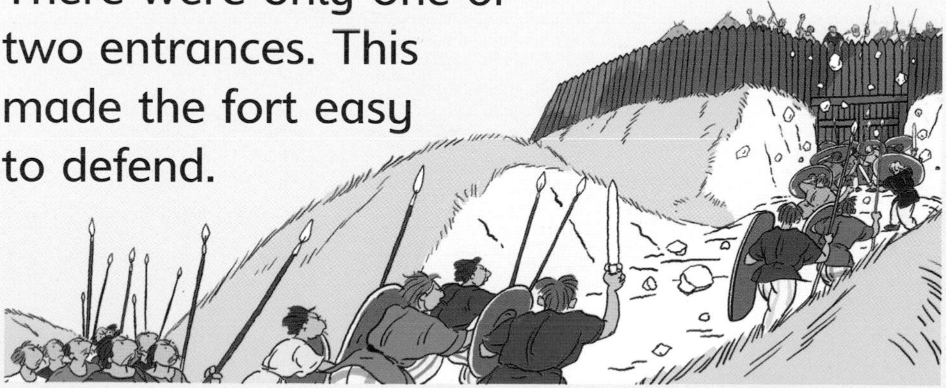

There were only one or two entrances. This made the fort easy to defend.

Village people

People lived in round houses inside the hillfort.

The walls of the house were made from sticks.

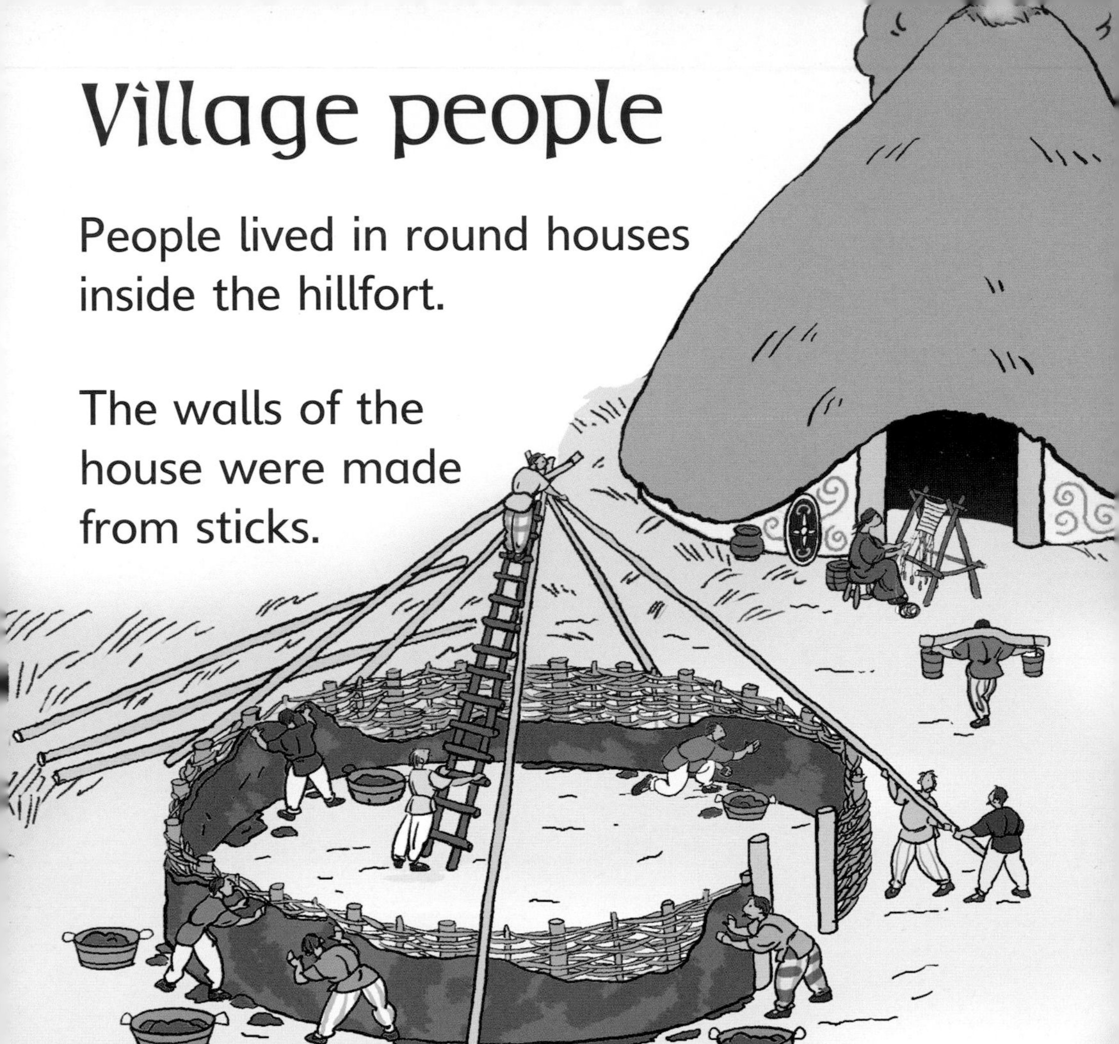

The sticks were covered with mud to keep out wind and rain.

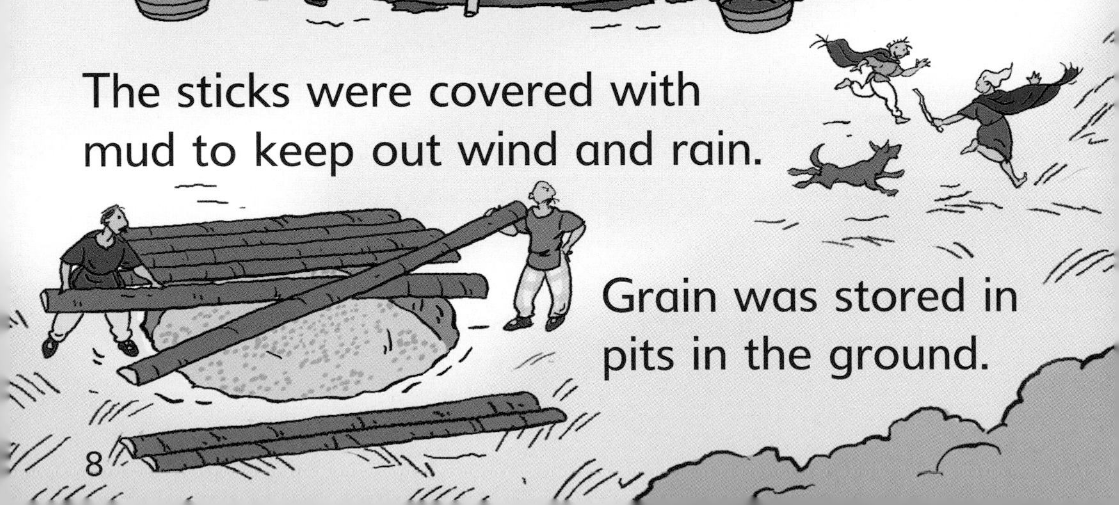

Grain was stored in pits in the ground.

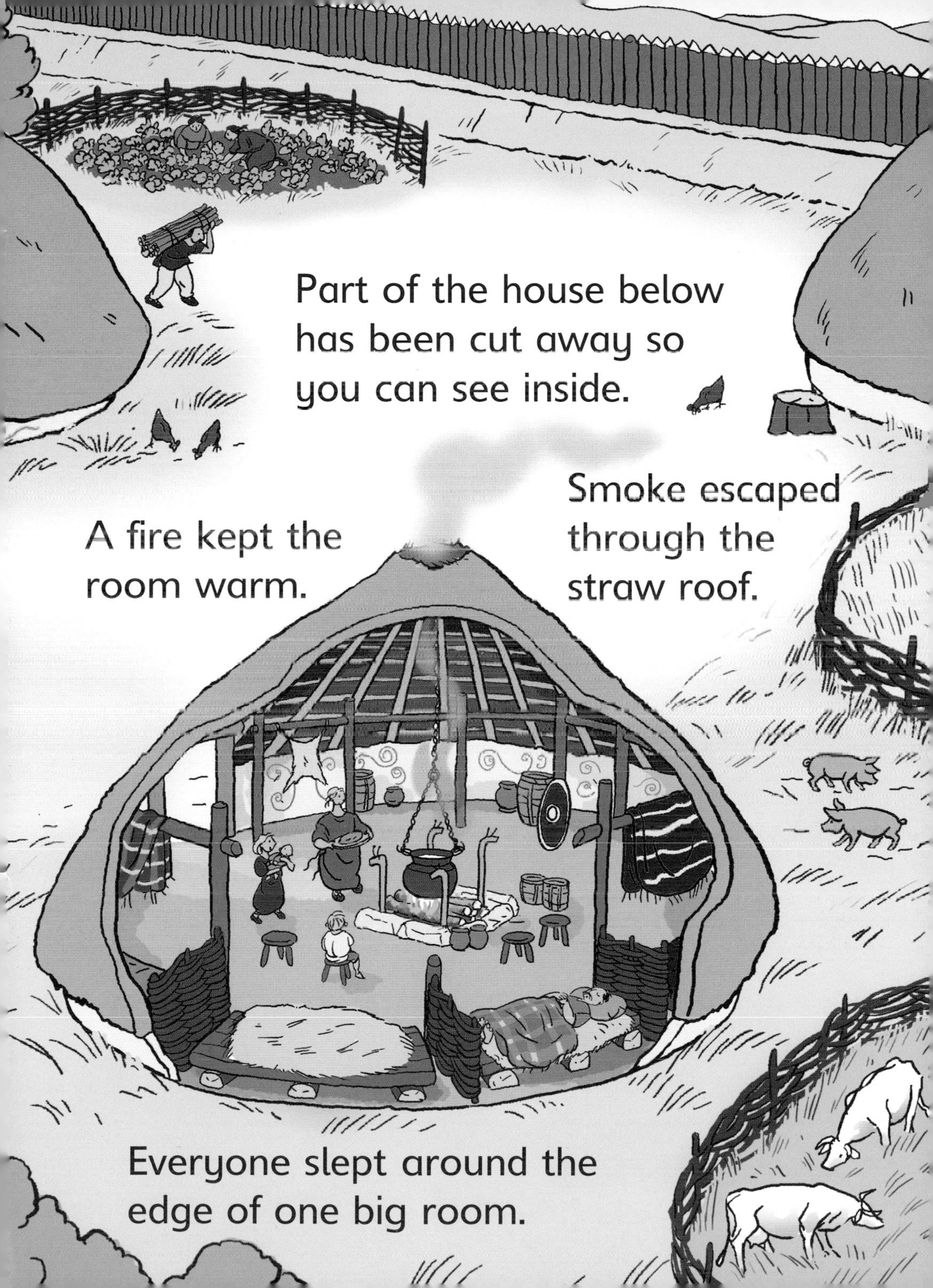

Part of the house below has been cut away so you can see inside.

A fire kept the room warm.

Smoke escaped through the straw roof.

Everyone slept around the edge of one big room.

Farming and food

The Celts grew oats, wheat and barley. They used them to make porridge and bread.

1. Men cut the wheat using iron tools called sickles.

2. Women ground the grain into flour between two stones.

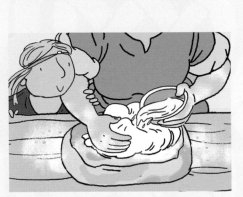

3. They mixed some water into the flour to make dough.

4. Then, they cooked the dough on a stone next to a fire.

The Celts had knives, but no forks - so they ate with their fingers.

Most meals were meat stews, vegetable stews, or porridge. The food was served from pots, jugs and pans like these ones.

Looking good

The Celts wanted their clothes to look good, as well as keep them warm.

Women used plants to dye wool, then wove it into patterned cloth.

Men wore tunics with baggy leggings and a belt. Women wore long dresses.

For extra warmth, people wore cloaks that were held in place with a brooch.

Celts liked wearing bracelets, and collars called torcs around their necks.

Only an important person would wear a gold torc like this one.

The ends of this torc can stretch apart to fit around a person's neck.

Very rich men brushed gold dust over their cloaks.

Crafty Celts

Celts were very good at making things from metal.

Bronze is a mixture of two metals, tin and copper. The Celts used it to make ornaments like this cow.

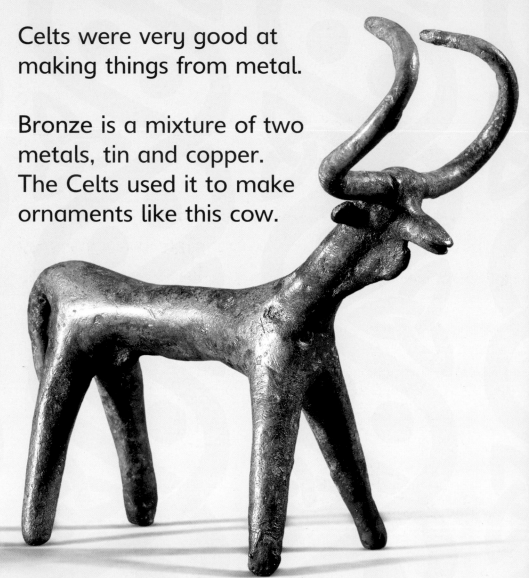

At first bronze is dark brown and shiny, but it turns green as it gets older.

14

1. A craftsman made a wax shape, then covered it in clay.

2. Then, he baked it to melt the wax and make the clay hard.

3. He poured out the wax, then poured in melted bronze.

4. The bronze set as it cooled then the clay was chipped off.

Gifts for the gods

The Celts believed in lots of different gods and goddesses. They tried to keep the gods happy by giving them gifts.

Druids collected gifts like weapons, tools and bronze brooches.

They put the gifts in a river or lake for the gods to find.

Druids sometimes killed people to give as gifts to the gods.

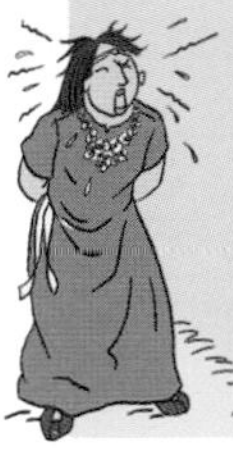

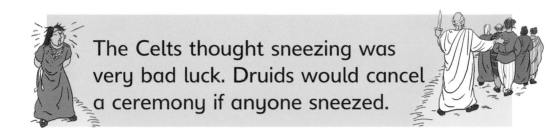

The Celts thought sneezing was very bad luck. Druids would cancel a ceremony if anyone sneezed.

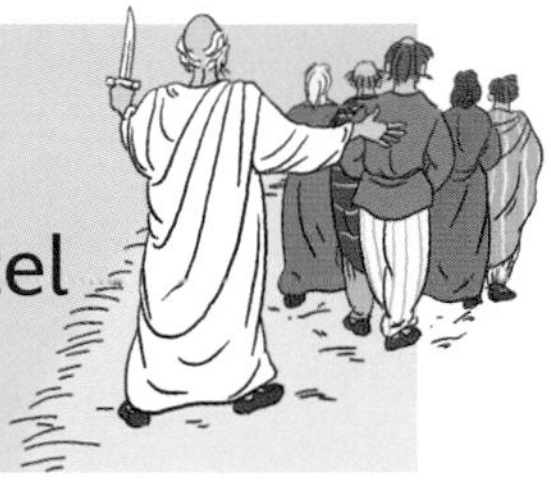

This is the body of a Celt who was found in a bog in Denmark. Many people think he was killed by druids.

The mud has stopped his body from rotting away.

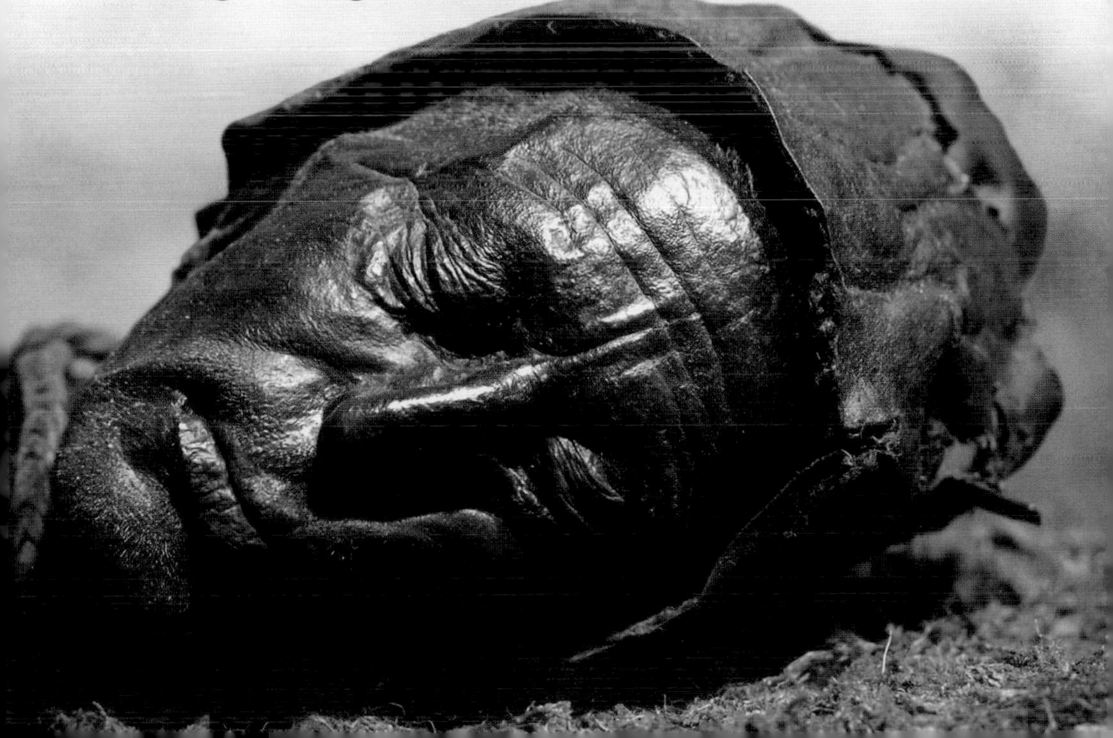

Festival fun

The Celts held festivals at different times of year to celebrate their gods and the seasons.

The Celts celebrated the end of winter with fires and feasts.

Men raced each other on horseback at the summer festival.

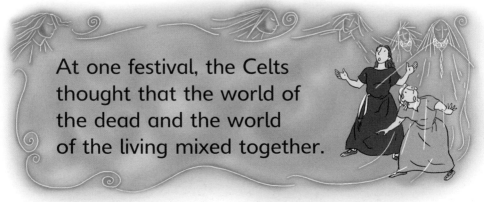

At one festival, the Celts thought that the world of the dead and the world of the living mixed together.

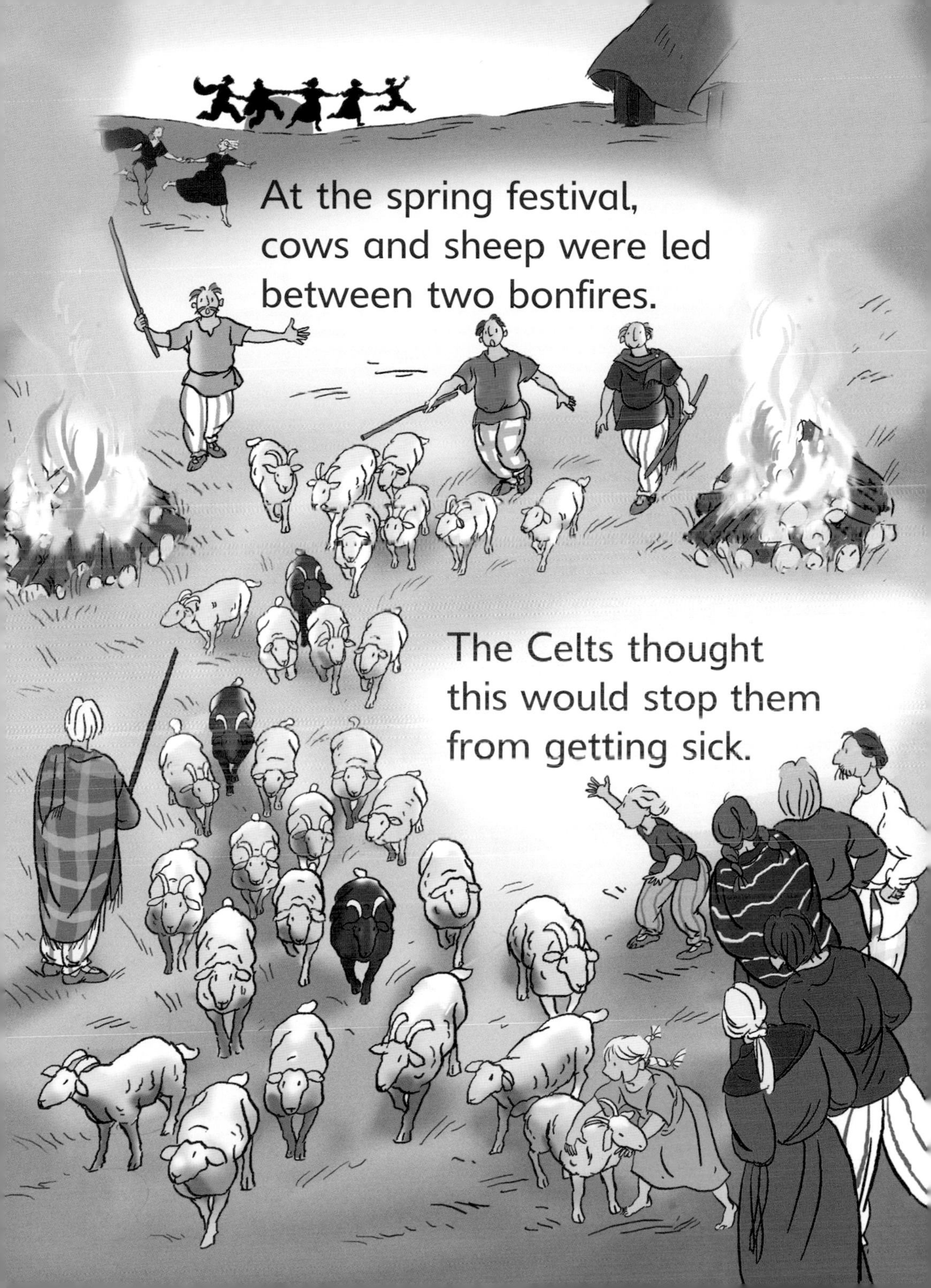

At the spring festival, cows and sheep were led between two bonfires.

The Celts thought this would stop them from getting sick.

Fearsome fighters

Celts were famous for being fierce, brave warriors. Different tribes sometimes fought to get each other's land.

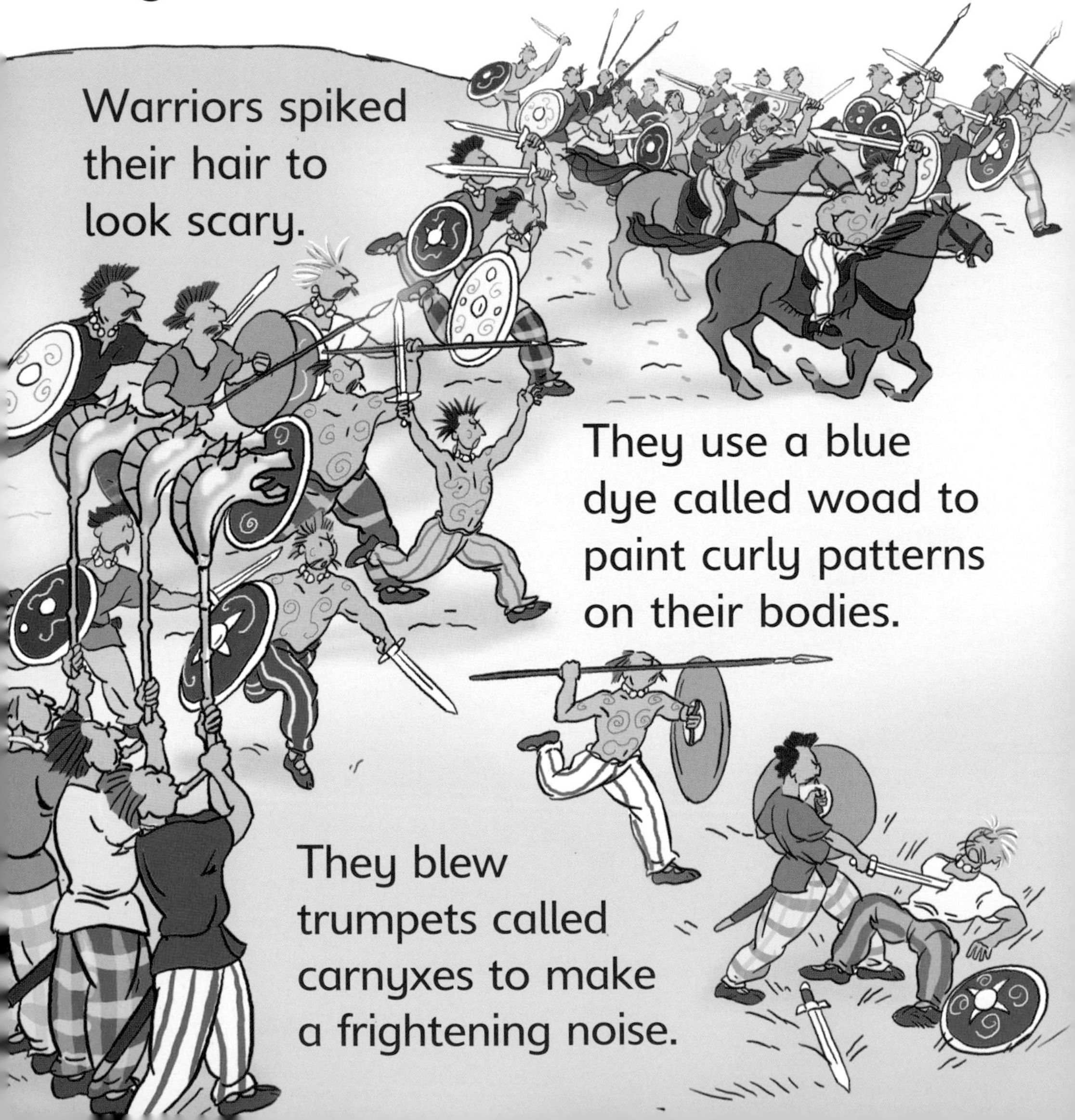

Warriors spiked their hair to look scary.

They use a blue dye called woad to paint curly patterns on their bodies.

They blew trumpets called carnyxes to make a frightening noise.

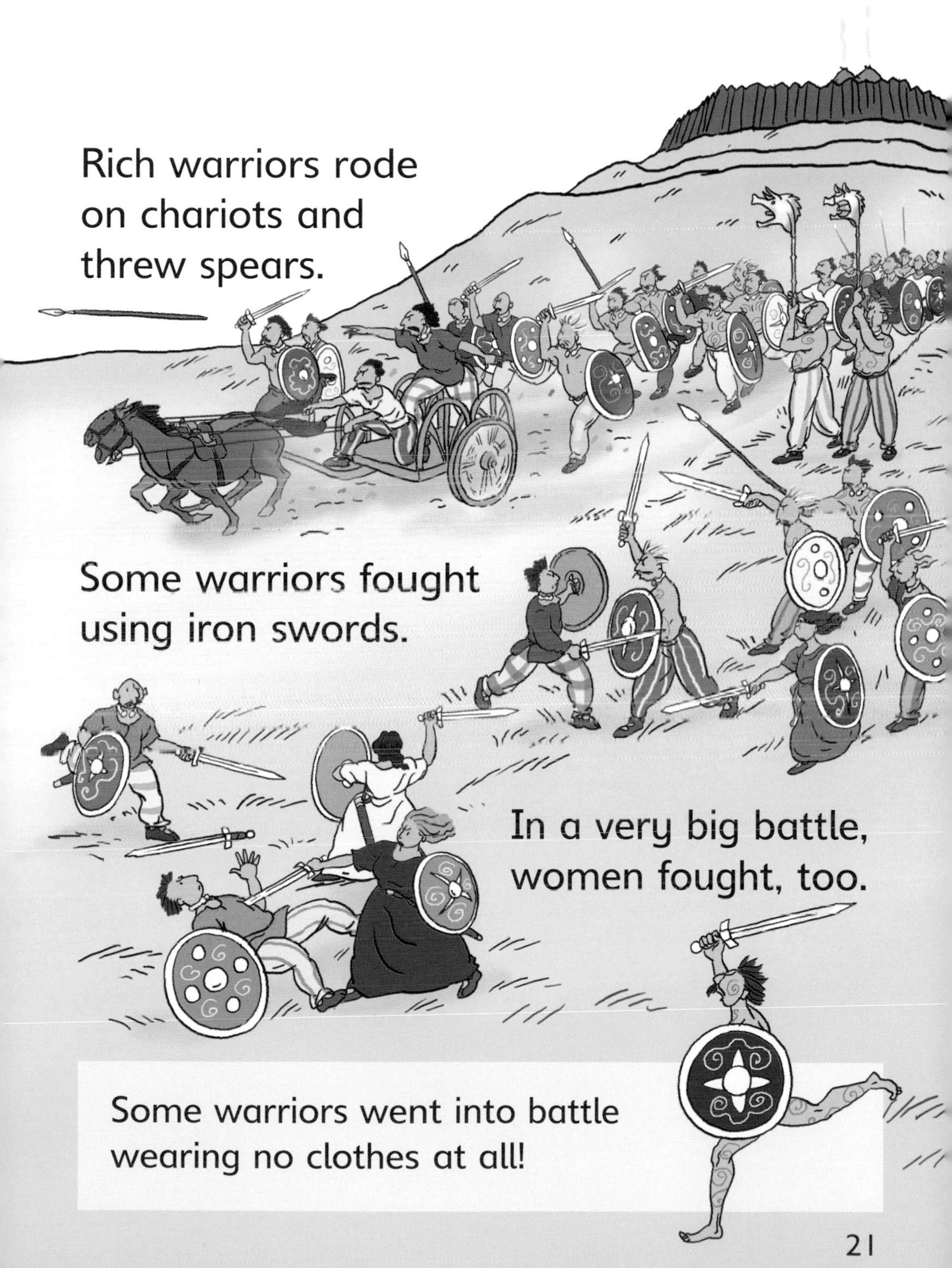

Rich warriors rode on chariots and threw spears.

Some warriors fought using iron swords.

In a very big battle, women fought, too.

Some warriors went into battle wearing no clothes at all!

Telling tales

Warriors often had a feast after winning a battle. After the feast, the men boasted to each other about how brave they were.

The bard did the chief's boasting for him...

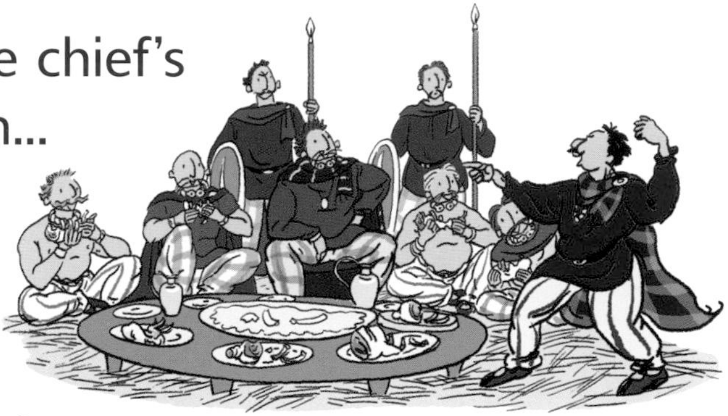

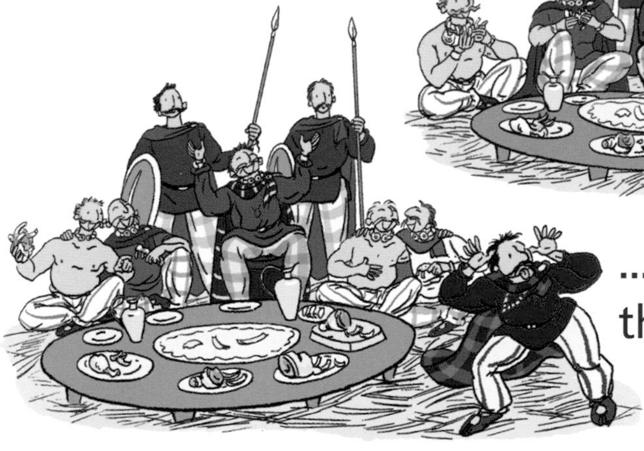

...and made fun of the chief's enemies.

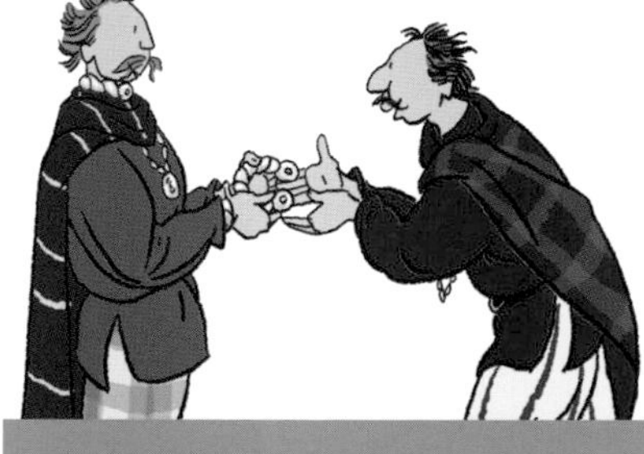

If the chief liked what he heard, then he rewarded the bard with gold.

A good bard could become very, very rich.

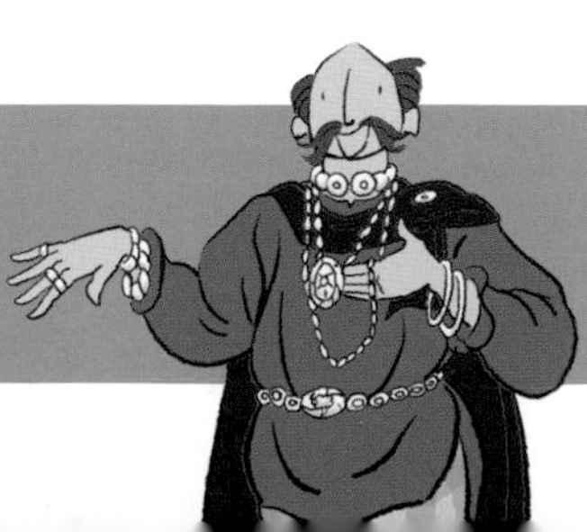

Bards also told stories and poems about famous warriors. This is an old painting of a famous Celtic warrior called Cu Chulainn.

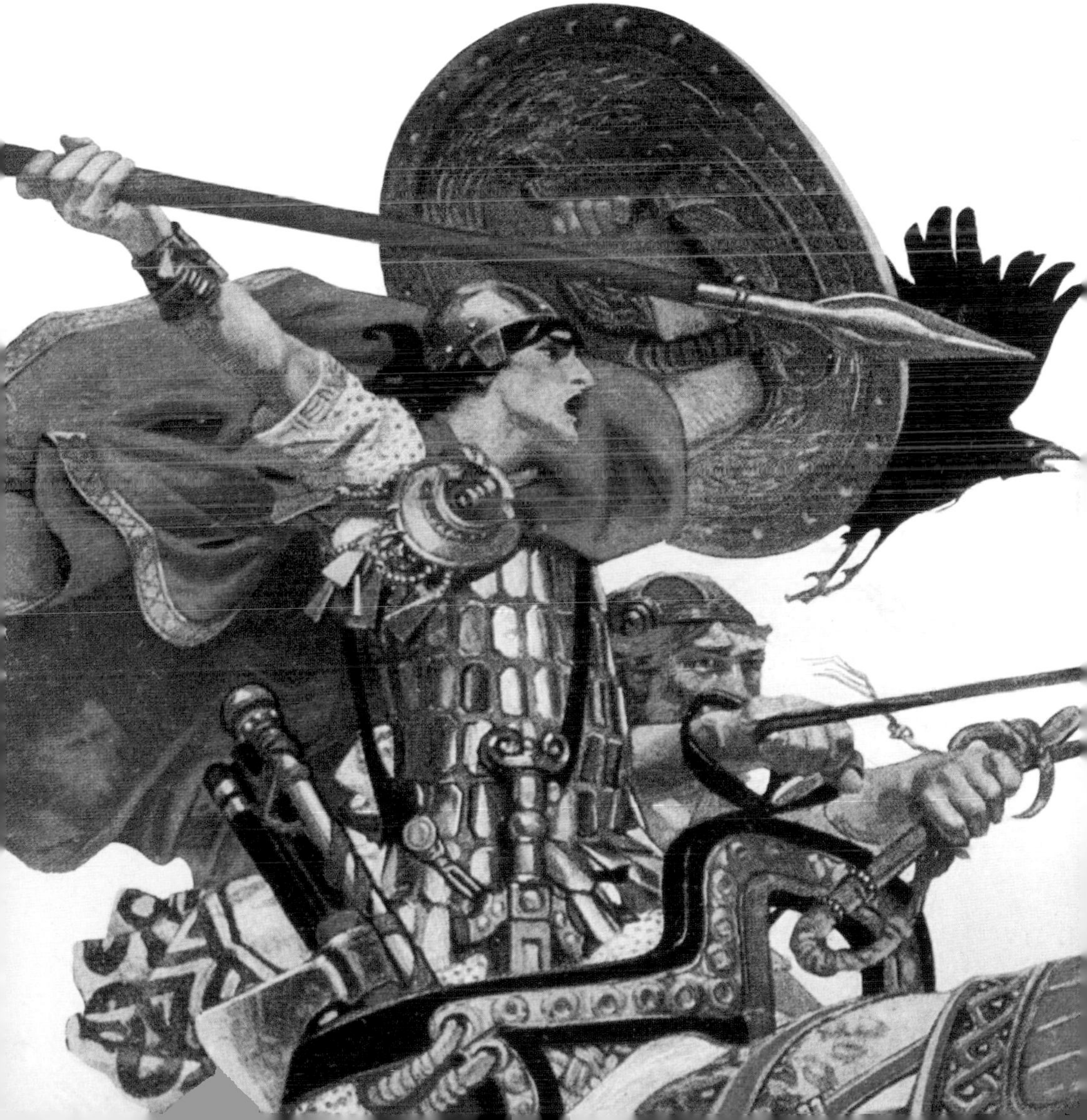

Trouble ahead

The Celts weren't the only people living in Europe. There were Greeks and Romans too.

The Romans were jealous when they saw that the Celts had such good farmland.

Julius Caesar led a large Roman army to attack the Celtic tribes in Gaul (now France).

Some of the tribes got together to fight back, but the Romans won in the end.

This is a statue of the leader of the Celtic tribes, Vercingetorix. He was killed by the Romans.

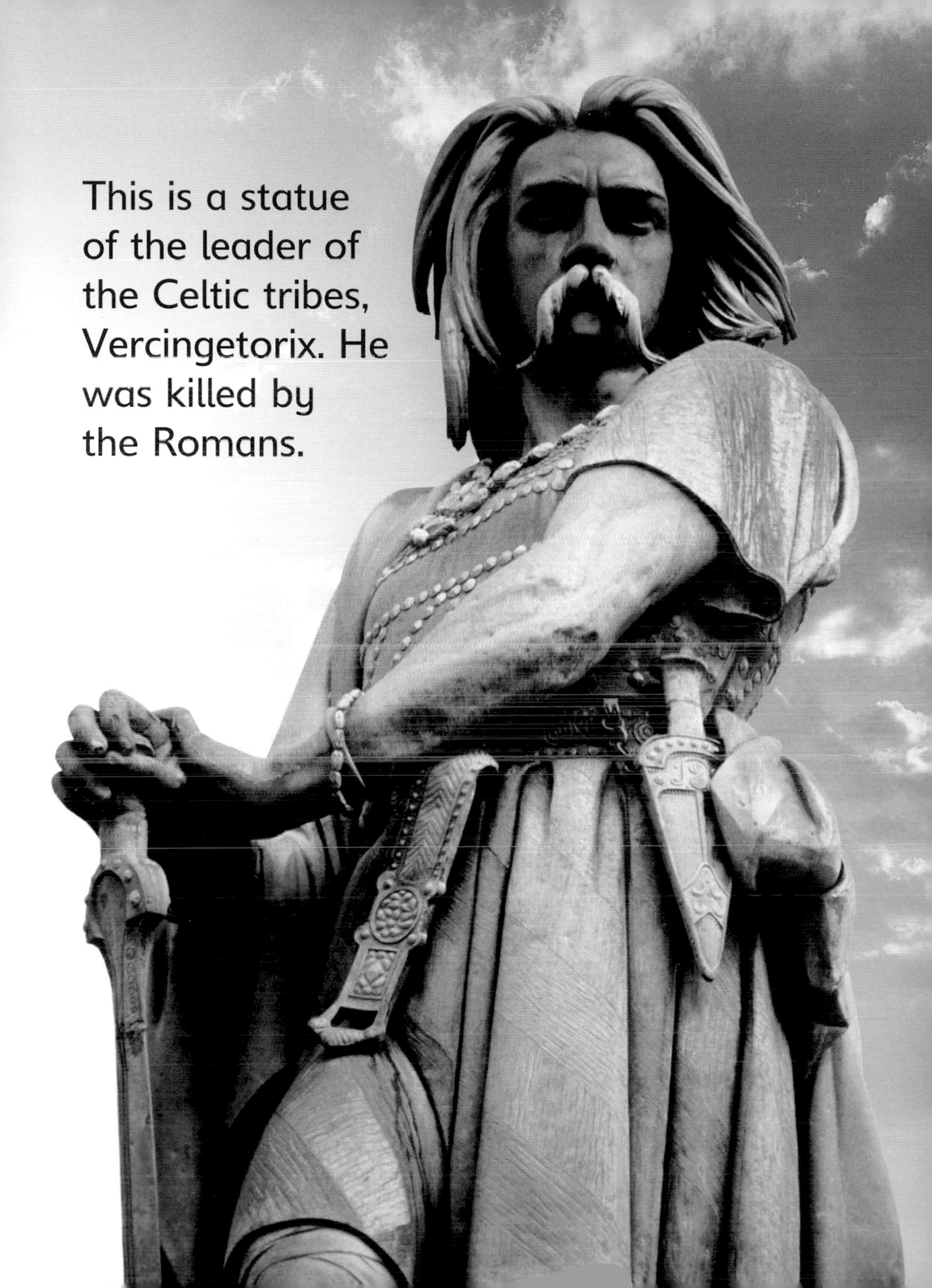

Battling Britain

The Romans also invaded Britain. Some tribes didn't like this and fought back.

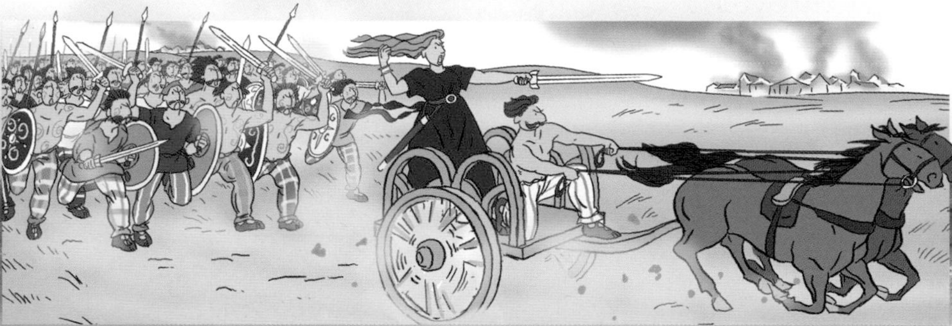

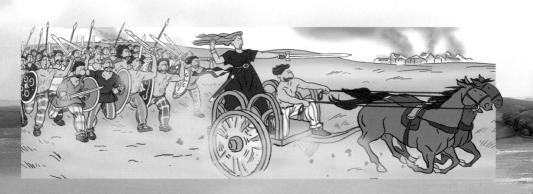

Queen Boudica and thousands of Celts attacked some Roman towns, but the Romans fought them and lots of Celts were killed.

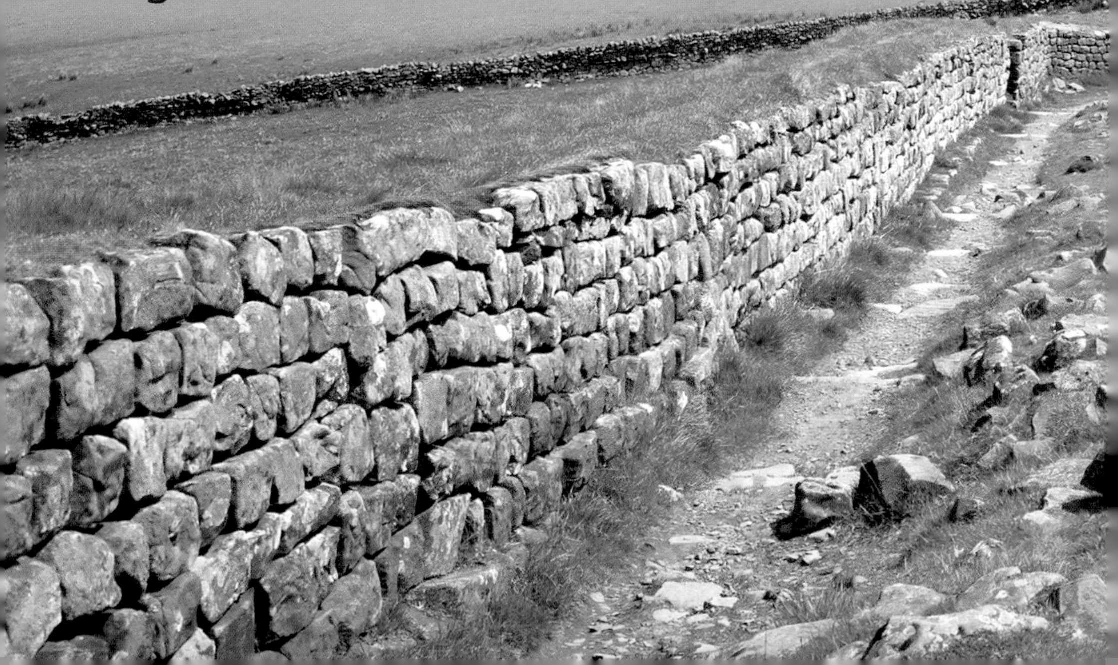

The Celts in England couldn't stop the Romans from taking over. But the Romans weren't able to take control of Scotland.

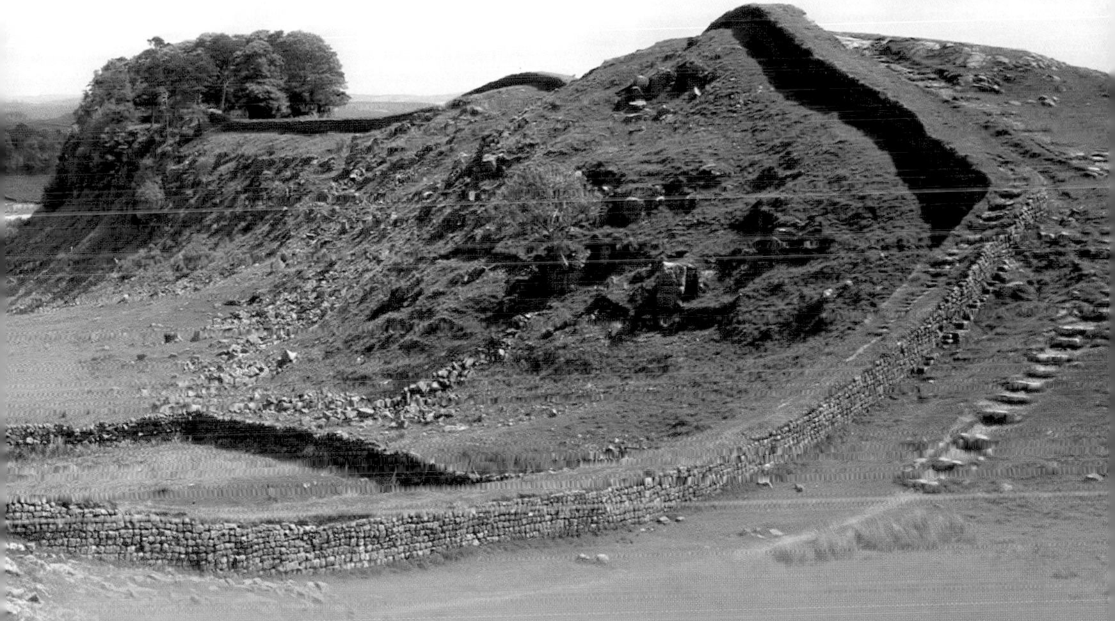

The Romans wanted to watch over the Celts in Scotland. They built this long wall, called Hadrian's wall, for soldiers to guard.

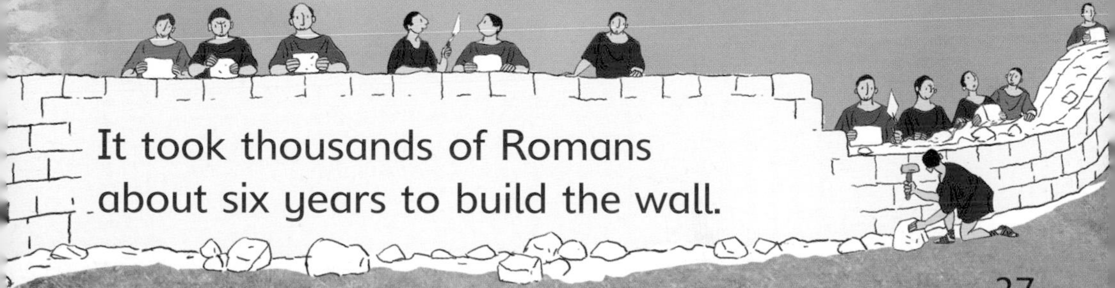

It took thousands of Romans about six years to build the wall.

Celtic clues

The Celts never wrote anything about themselves. People who study them have to use other clues to find out about them.

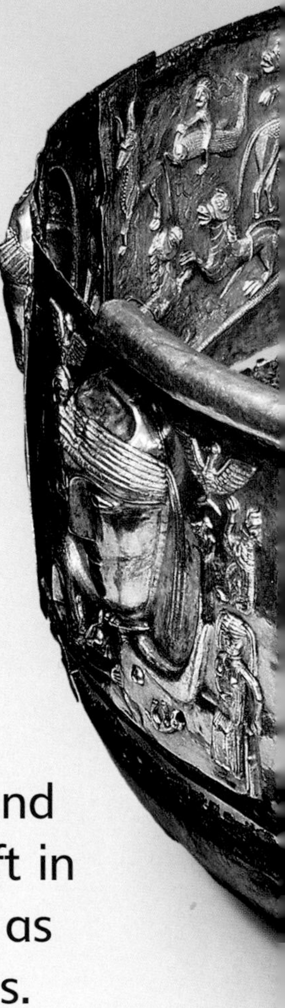

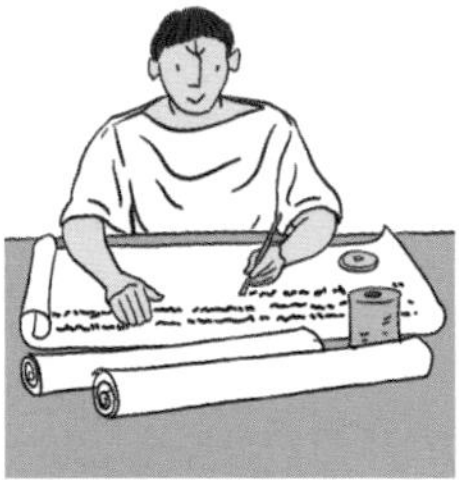

The Romans were interested in how the Celts lived and wrote lots about them.

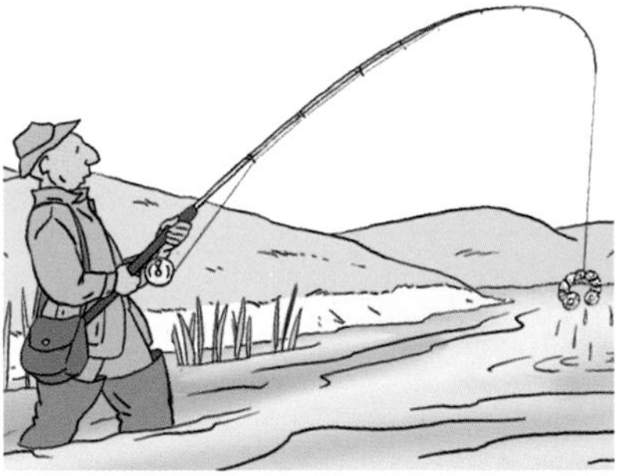

People have found Celtic objects left in rivers and lakes as gifts for the gods.

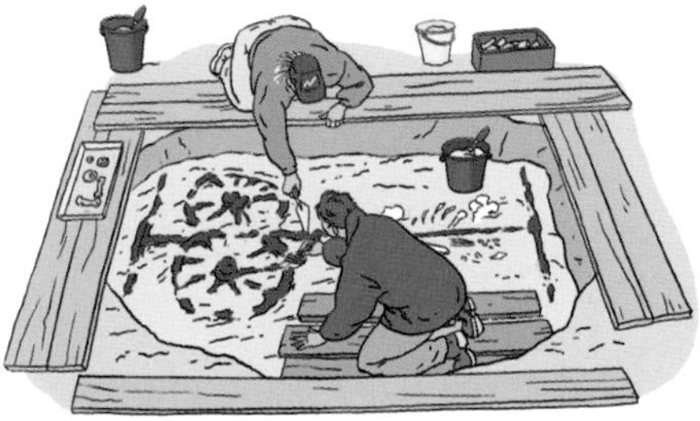

Sometimes Celts were buried with chariots, weapons and other things.

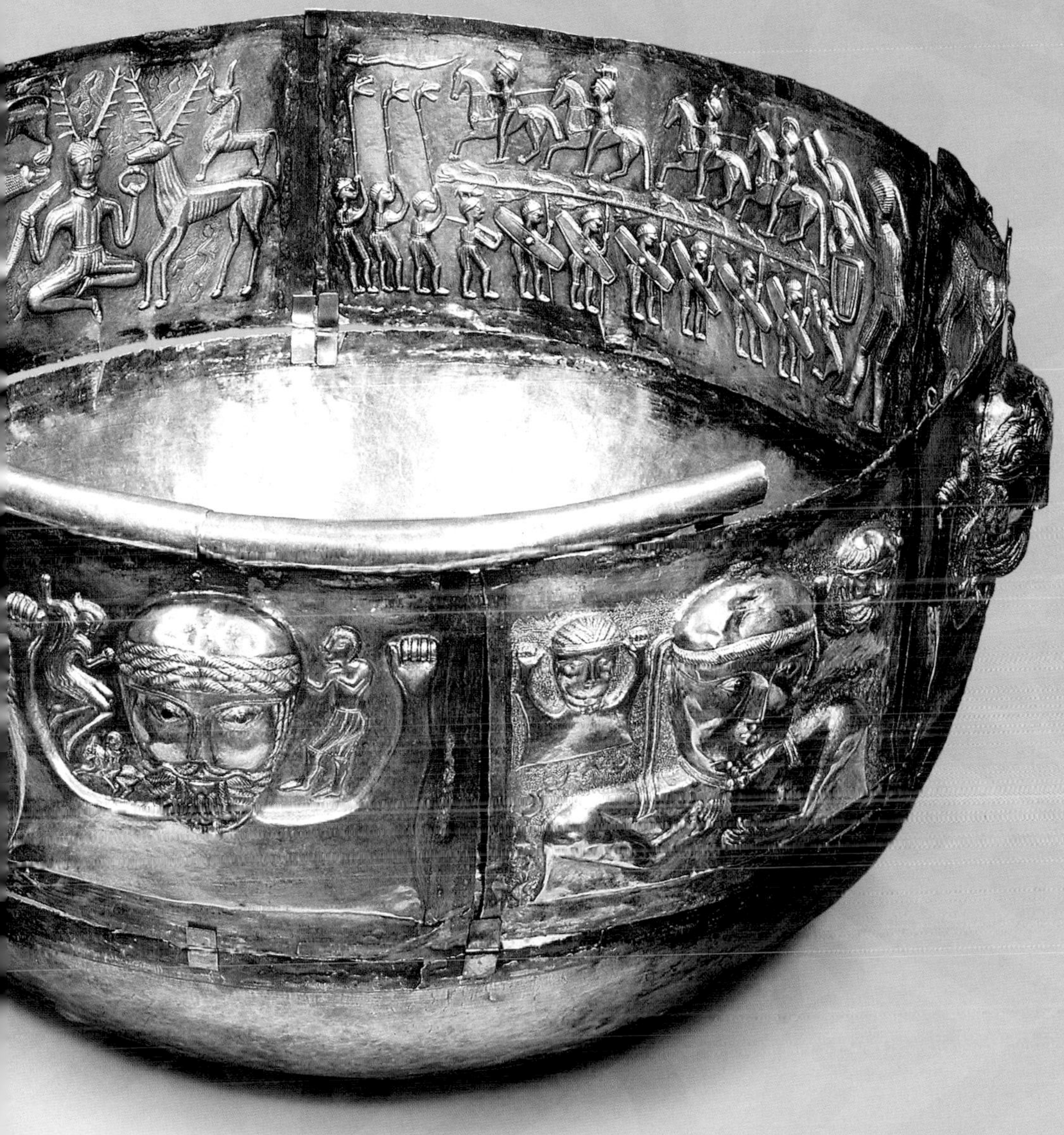

This Celtic bowl has pictures around it showing people hunting and fighting. The big heads on the outside are gods.

Glossary of Celtic words

Here are some of the words in this book you might not know. This page tells you what they mean.

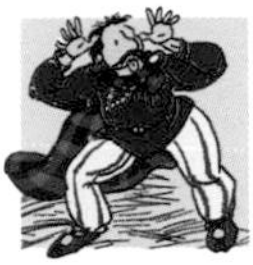

bard - a man who made up stories and poems and sang songs.

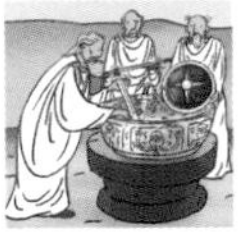

druid - a Celtic priest. Druids were very wise and important.

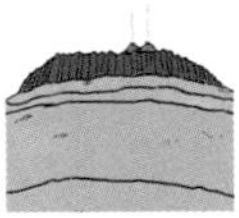

hillfort - a village with a wooden fence around it, built on top of a hill.

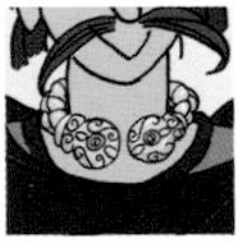

torc - a gold, silver or bronze collar that Celts wore around their necks.

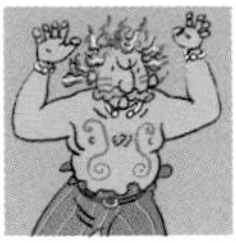

woad - blue dye. Celts used woad to paint their bodies and dye clothes.

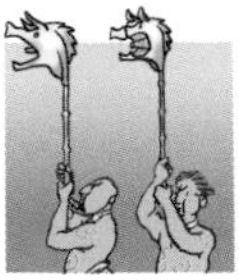

carnyx - a tall war trumpet. Warriors blew carnyxes to scare their enemies.

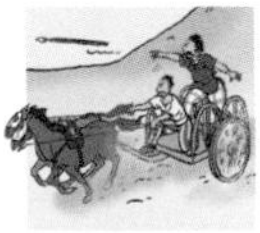

chariot – a cart pulled by two horses. Rich warriors rode chariots into battle.

Websites to visit

You can visit exciting websites to find out more about Celts.

To visit these websites, go to the Usborne Quicklinks Website as **www.usborne-quicklinks.com** Read the internet safety guidelines, and then type the keywords "**beginners celts**".

The websites are regularly reviewed and the links in Usborne Quicklinks are updated. However, Usborne Publishing is not responsible, and does not accept liability, for the content or availability of any website other than its own. We recommend that children are supervised while on the internet.

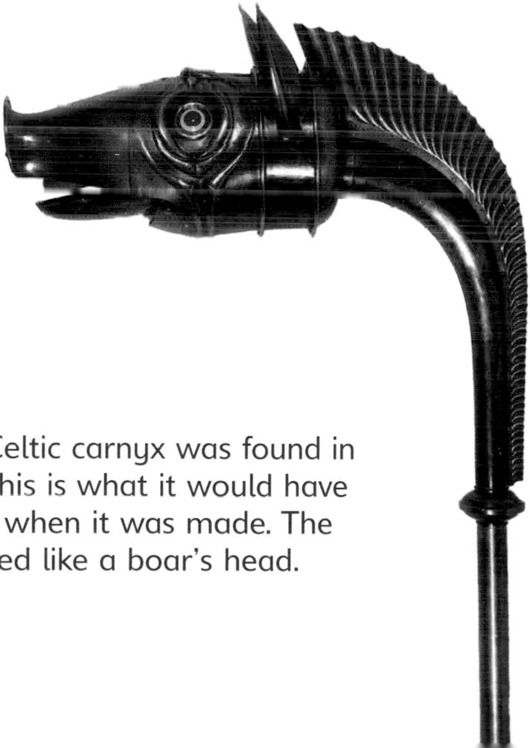

A broken Celtic carnyx was found in Scotland. This is what it would have looked like when it was made. The top is shaped like a boar's head.

Index

bards, 4, 22-23, 30

Boudica, 26

carnyxes, 20, 30, 31

chariots, 21, 28, 30

crops, 5, 10

druids, 4, 16-17, 30

dye, 12, 20, 30

Europe, 3, 24

feasts, 18, 22

festivals, 18-19

gods and goddesses, 16, 18, 28, 29

hillforts, 6-7, 8, 30

Iron Age, 3

Romans, 24, 25, 26, 27, 28

round houses, 8-9

tools, 3, 10, 16

torcs, 13, 30

tribes, 4-5, 6, 7, 20, 24, 25, 26

Vercingetorix, 25

warriors, 4, 20-21, 22, 23, 30

weapons, 3, 16, 21, 28

woad, 20, 30

Acknowledgements

Photographic manipulation by John Russell

Photo credits

The publishers are grateful to the following for permission to reproduce material: Cover © Heritage Image Partnership Ltd / Alamy; p1 © C M Dixon/HIP/Topfoto; p6-7 © Jason Hawkes/ CORBIS; p10-11 © The British Museum/HIP/Topfoto; p12-13 © The British Museum/HIP/ Topfoto; p14-15 © akg-images/Erich Lessing; p16-17 © Chris Lisle/Corbis; p22-23 © Mary Evans Picture Library/Alamy; p24-25 © R. Sheridan/Ancient Art and Architecture Collection Ltd; p26-27 © Robert Harding Picture Library/Alamy; p28-29 © Topfoto/HIP; p30-31 © National Museums of Scotland.

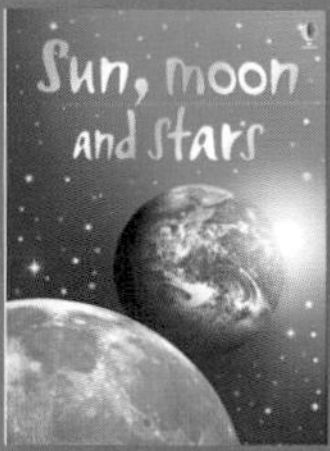
Sun, moon and stars
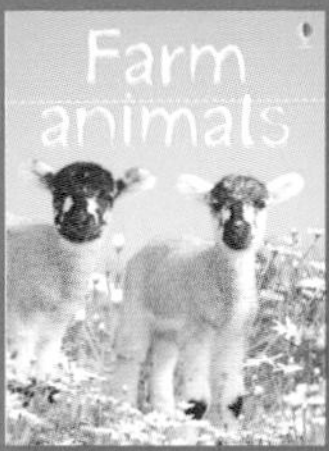
Farm animals
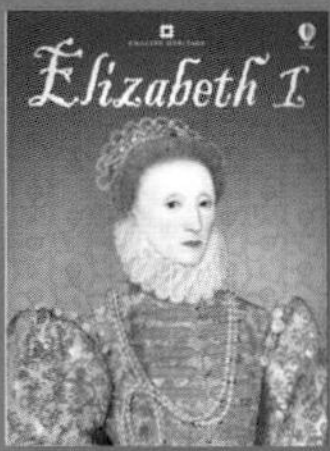
Elizabeth I
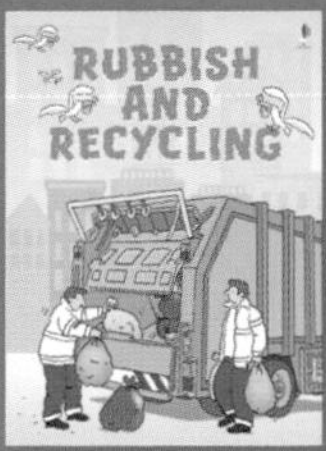
RUBBISH AND RECYCLING
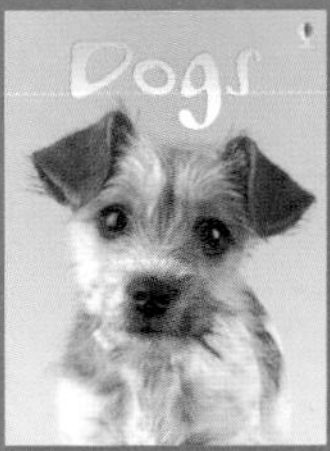
Dogs
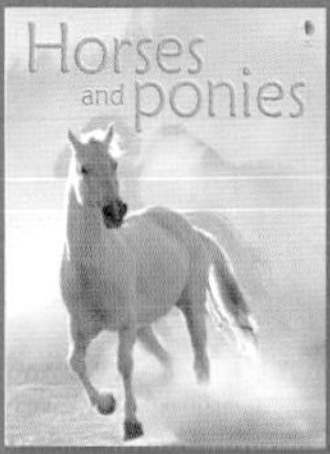
Horses and ponies
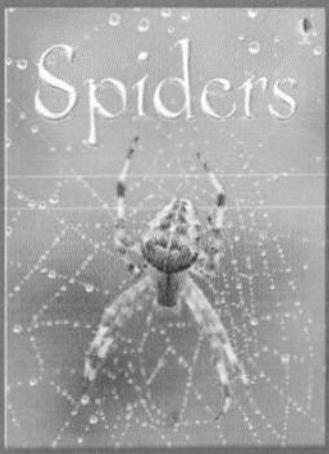
Spiders
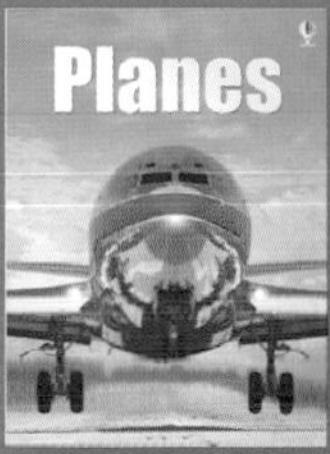
Planes
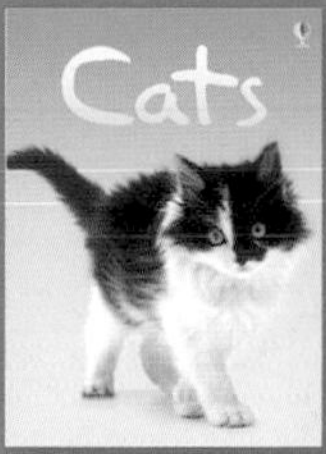
Cats
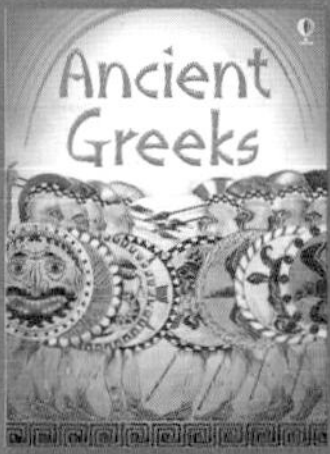
Ancient Greeks
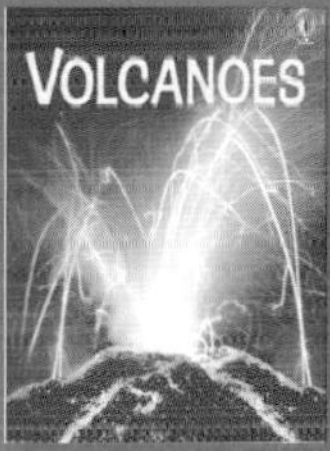
VOLCANOES
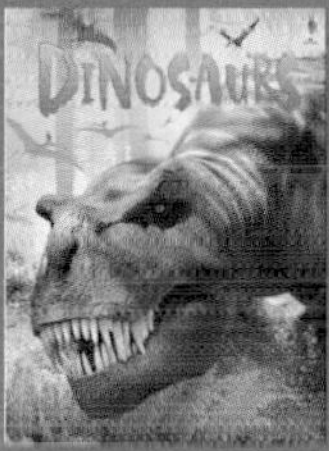
DINOSAURS
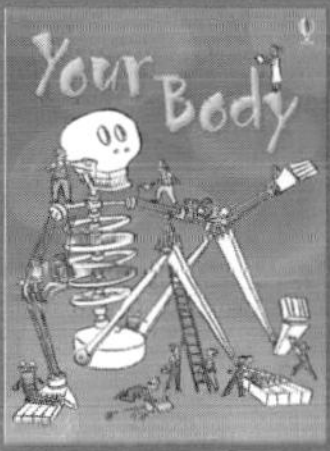
Your Body
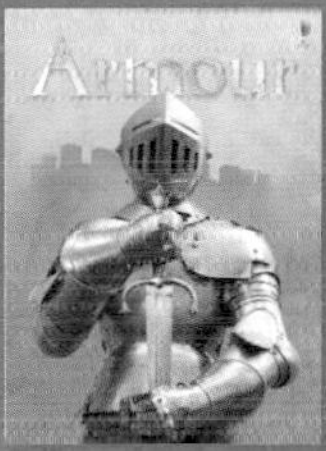
Armour
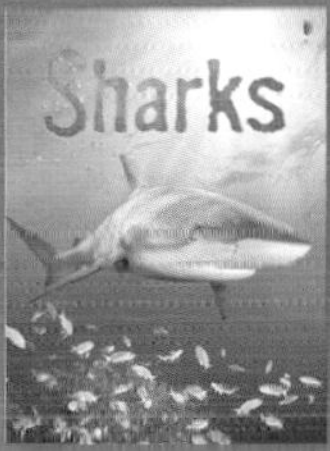
Sharks
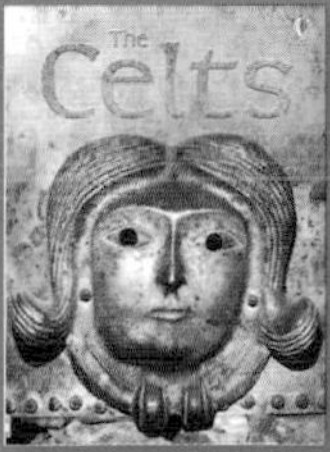
The Celts
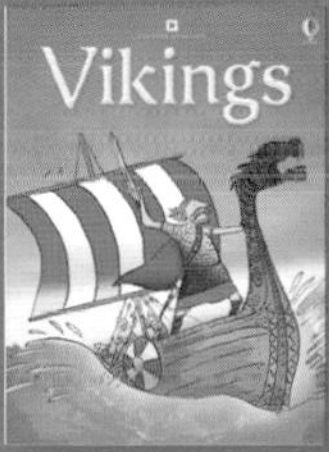
Vikings
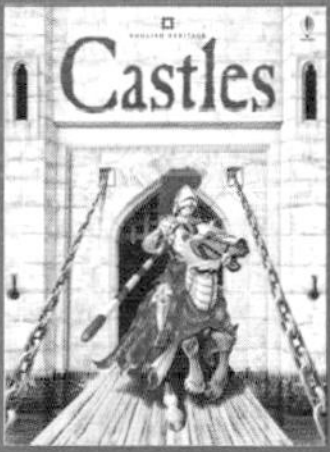
Castles
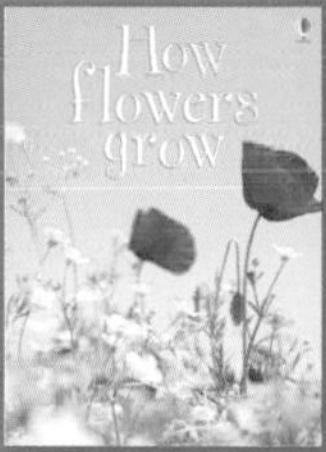
How flowers grow
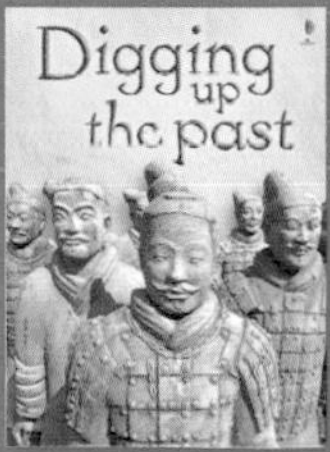
Digging up the past
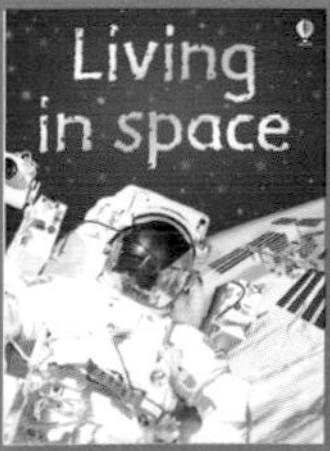
Living in space
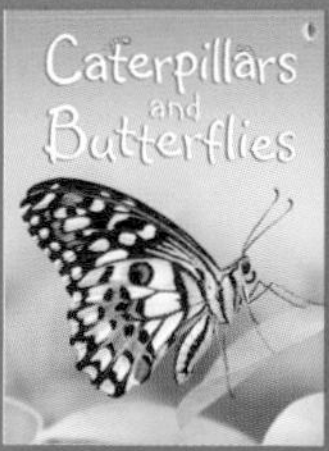
Caterpillars and Butterflies
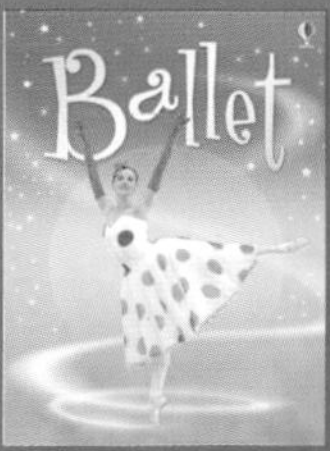
Ballet
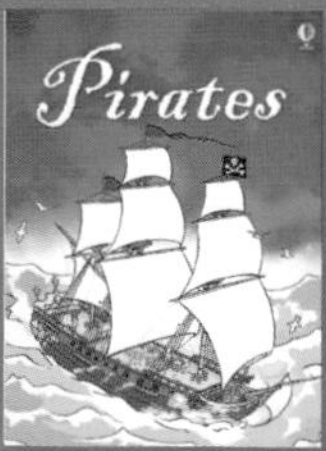
Pirates
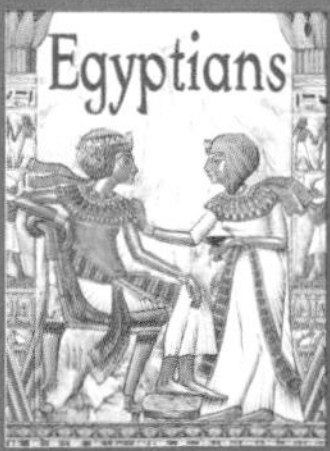
Egyptians

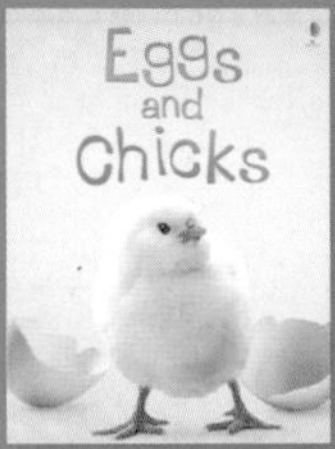
Eggs and Chicks
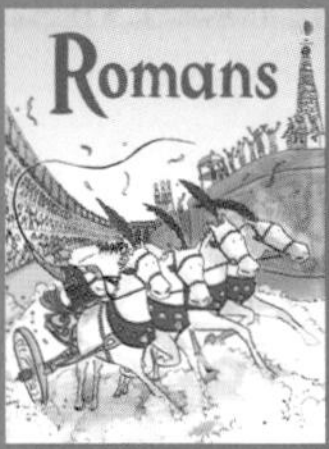
Romans
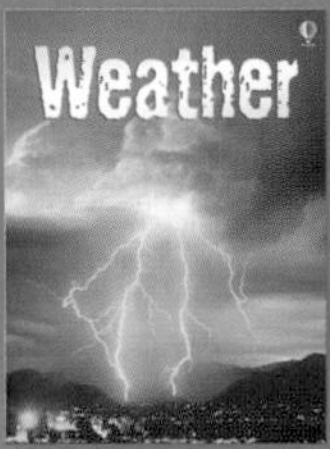
Weather
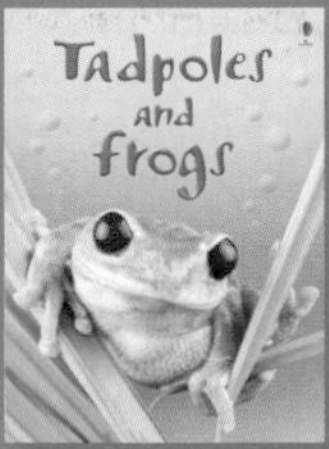
Tadpoles and frogs
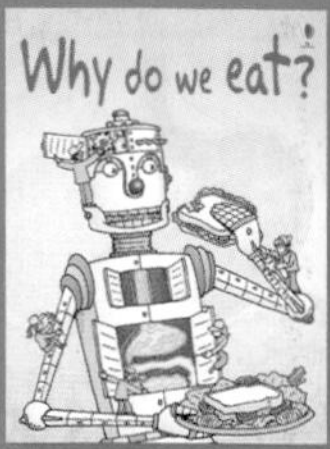
Why do we eat?
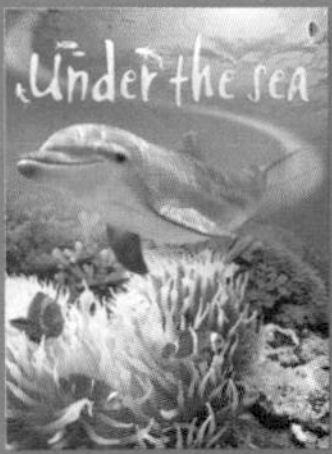
Under the sea
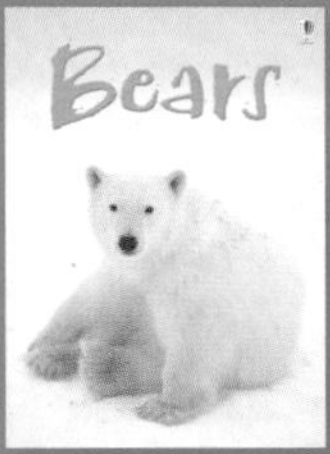
Bears
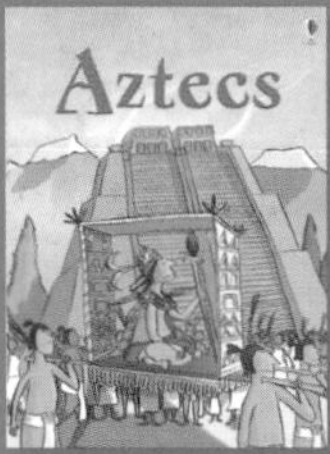
Aztecs
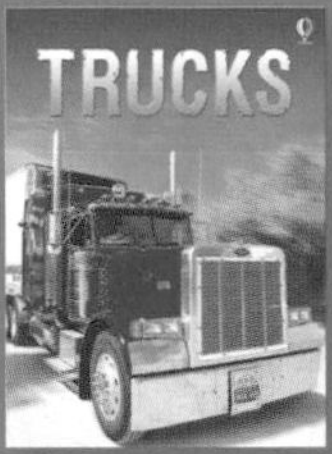
TRUCKS
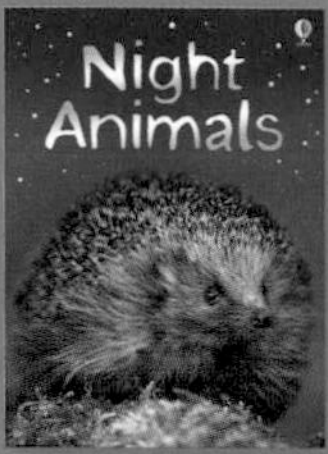
Night Animals
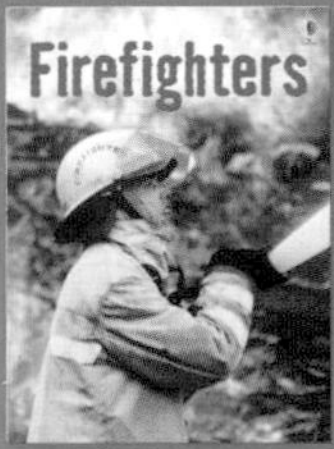
Firefighters
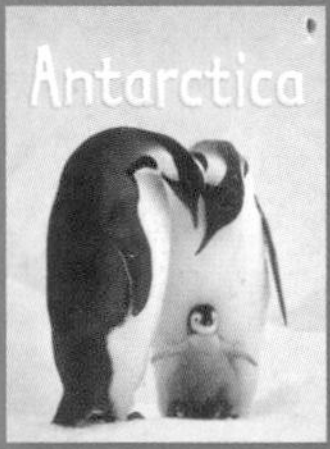
Antarctica
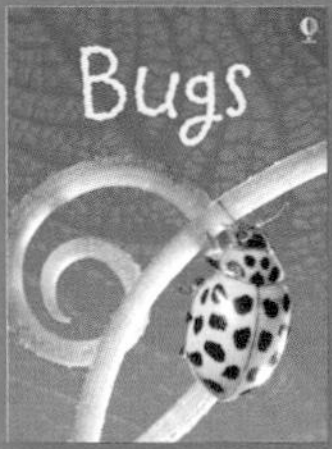
Bugs
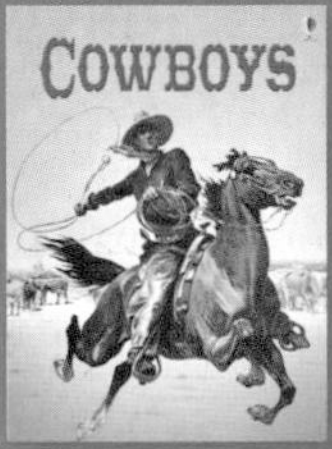
COWBOYS
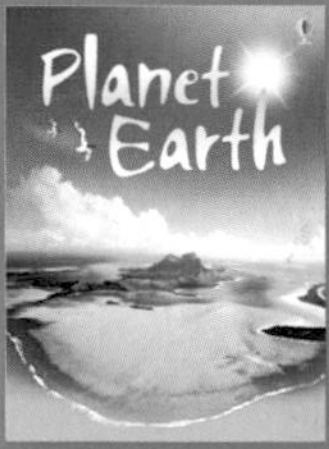
Planet Earth
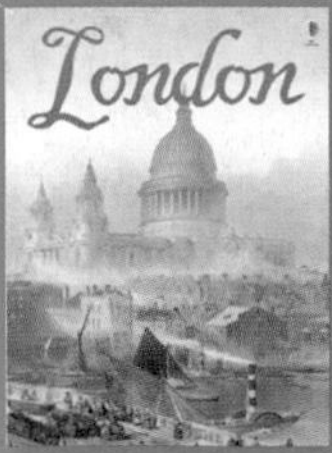
London
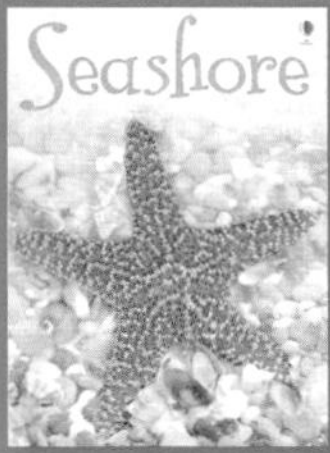
Seashore
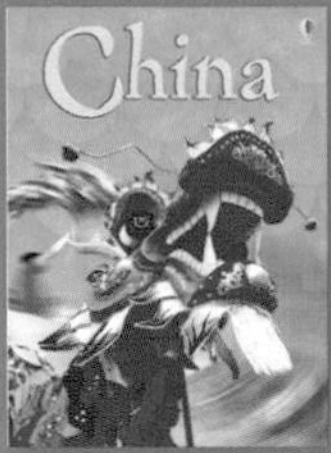
China
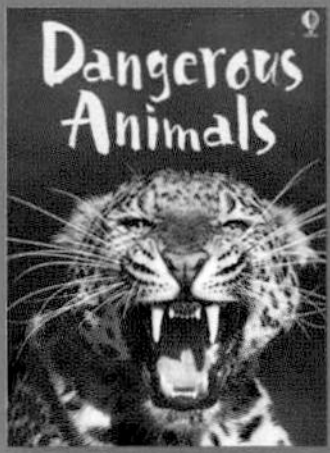
Dangerous Animals
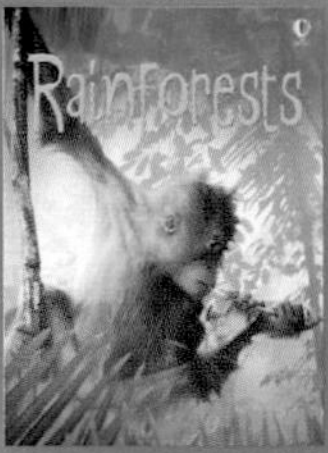
Rainforests
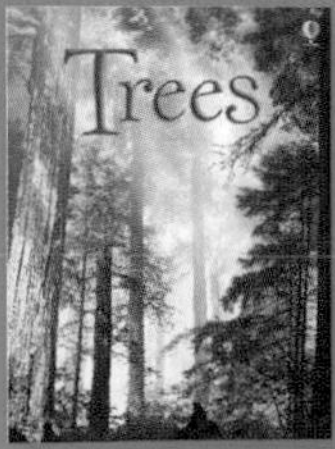
Trees
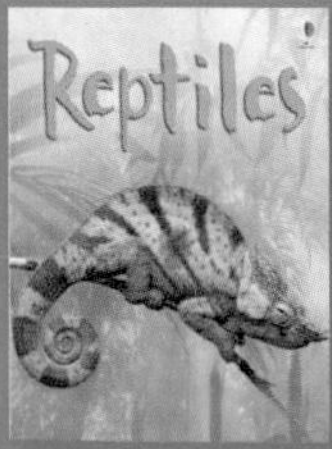
Reptiles
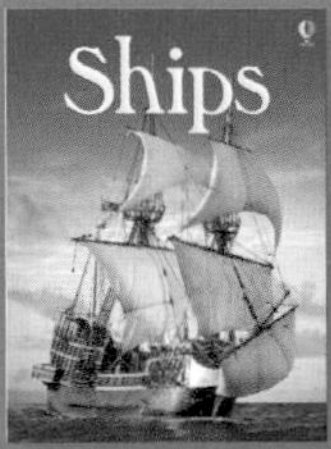
Ships
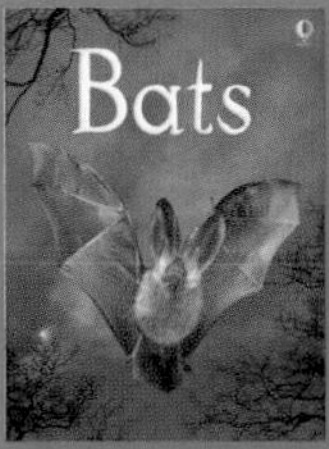
Bats
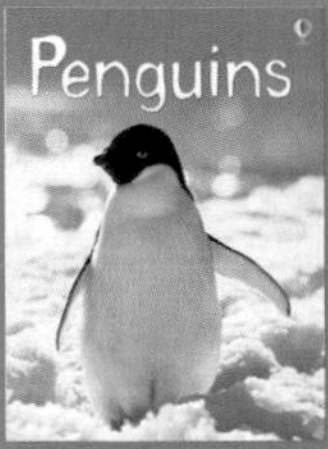
Penguins